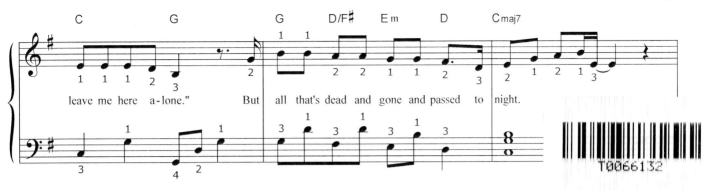

leave me here a-lone." But all that's dead and gone and passed to night.

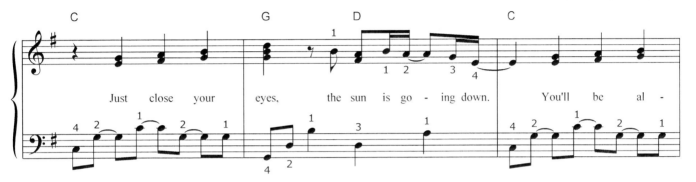

Just close your eyes, the sun is go - ing down. You'll be al -

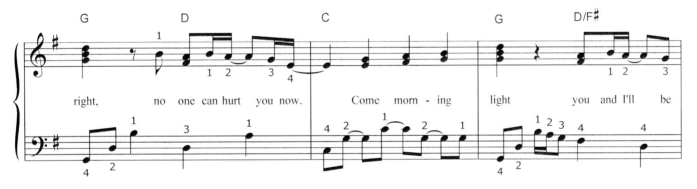

right, no one can hurt you now. Come morn - ing light you and I'll be

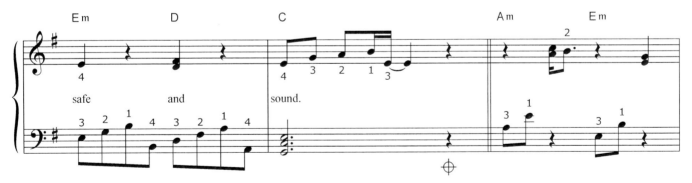

safe and sound.

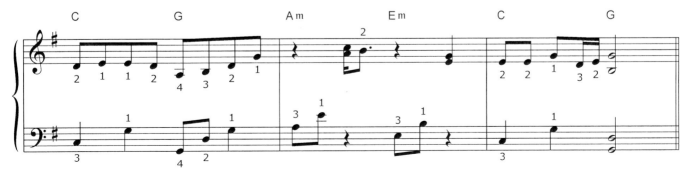

3

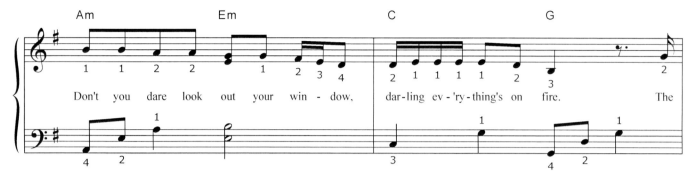

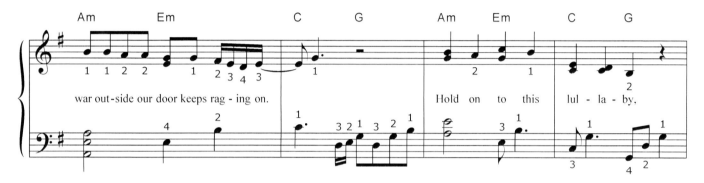

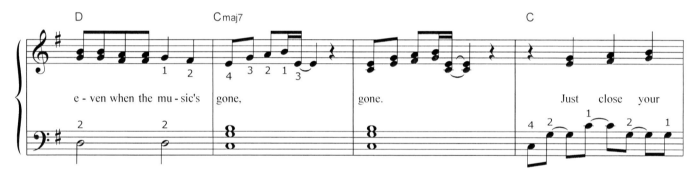

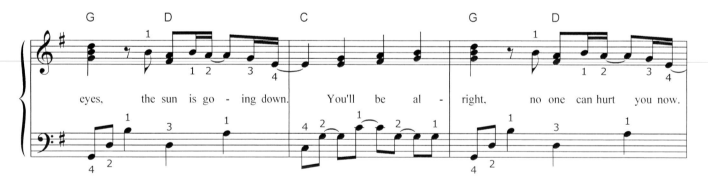

4

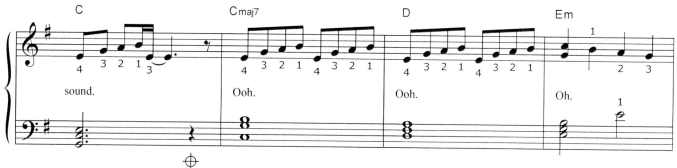

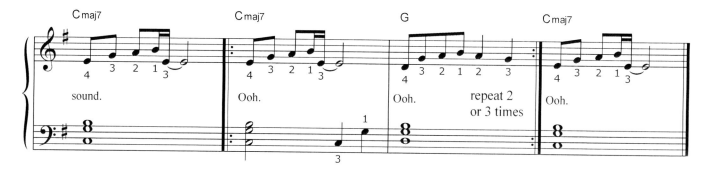

Published by Woods Music & Books, Inc.
P.O. Box 223434, Princeville, HI 96722 U.S.A.

© 2012 by Sylvia Woods

www.harpcenter.com

ISBN 978-0-936661-54-4